Sexual Assault

Healing Steps for Victims

David Powlison

New
Growth
Press

www.newgrowthpress.com

New Growth Press, Greensboro, NC 27404
Copyright © 2010 by Christian Counseling & Educational Foundation
All rights reserved. Published 2010.

Cover Design: Tandem Creative, Tom Temple, tandemcreative.net
Typesetting: Robin Black, www.blackbirdcreative.biz

ISBN-10: 1-935273-78-7
ISBN-13: 978-1-935273-78-3

Library of Congress Cataloging-in-Publication Data

Powlison, David, 1949-
    Sexual assault : healing steps for victims / David Powlison.
        p. cm.
    Includes bibliographical references and index.
    ISBN-13: 978-1-935273-78-3 (alk. paper)
    ISBN-10: 1-935273-78-7 (alk. paper)
    1. Abused women—Religious life. 2. Rape—Religious aspects—Christianity. 3. Rape victims—Religious life. 4. Sexual abuse victims—Religious life. 5. Rape victims—Psychology.
I. Title.
    BV4596.A2P69 2010
    248.8'6—dc22

                                                2010023096
Printed in Canada

21 20 19 18 17 16 15 14   5 6 7 8 9

Sexual assault is an invasive event of traumatic evil. You were victimized, and now you are suffering.

Before we talk about anything else, you need to know that God is extremely tender toward victims. Many psalms are the heart cries of those who suffer at the hands of others. The broken, the needy, the poor, the afflicted, the helpless, and the innocent pour forth words describing their experiences. You, too, can pour out your heart. God hears. The God and Father of Jesus Christ cares. You too are on his heart.

He cares about your experience of grave stress and evil. His own Son, although he didn't experience violence in a sexual form, was a victim of violent assault. No matter how awful your attack, no matter how long and slow your recovery, God is your Redeemer. He is able to redeem terrible wrongs and make them right. "He heals the brokenhearted and binds up their wounds" (Psalm 147:3). He is willing and able to make broken things whole. He is able to help you.

What Is Sexual Assault?

Sexual assault is a crime of power, domination, and control that uses sex. If you haven't already reported your assault to the police and sought medical help, please do so. If your assault happened a long time ago and you are not sure how to handle that, find a trusted friend, counselor, or pastor to talk through what your next steps should be. This minibook is written to help you rebuild. Getting appropriate legal and medical help is one step to getting the practical care you need.

Sexual assault is not only a crime in the legal sense, it is an evil before the face of God. It is an act of extreme violence and aggression. The strong overpower the weak.

Sexual assault is a life-changing event. A violent assault awakens some of the most painful, horrifying emotions that humans are capable of. Terror, shock, unbearable pain, overwhelming helplessness, and vulnerability are just some of the feelings you may experience. Such powerful feelings don't just go away. They affect every area of your life. Here are some ways that sexual assault victims typically suffer and struggle:

- **Numbness.** Life can feel unreal. "Normal" doesn't feel natural when something so wrong has happened.

- **Fear.** Most likely you are haunted by fears—
  of your memories, of people, of being alone, of
  dating, of intimacy.
- **Worry.** You might have some concrete worries—
  sexually transmitted diseases and pregnancy are
  two possible ones.
- **Anger.** This is an entirely appropriate response
  to the great evil you suffered. But when anger
  gets infected, then bitterness and hatred can
  become all-consuming and destructive.
- **Relationships.** Your relationships are affected.
  Perhaps you are having a hard time trusting anyone. Who do you tell? How much do you tell?
  Who can help?
- **Shame.** Even though you were the one who was
  victimized, it's common to feel a deep sense of
  shame and uncleanness. You feel dirtied by the
  evil of another.
- **Regret and Self Blame.** You might be think-
  ing, *If only…* (If only I hadn't done this…If only
  I hadn't been in that place) and *Why did I…?*
  (Why did I do that? Why didn't I do this?)

- **Nightmares and Flashbacks.** Specific places and events might trigger a flashback to the sexual assault. You might relive what happened in terrifying dreams.
- **Depression.** You might experience sadness that just doesn't go away. Life can seem meaningless after you have suffered traumatic evil.
- **Escapism.** You might try to forget what happened to you by using different forms of self-medication—drugs, alcohol, food, television.
- **Helplessness and Powerlessness.** No one intervened to help you. You can't rewind the tape and press erase.
- **Pain.** You hurt on many levels. The pain can feel unbearable.

The Scope of the Problem

Sexual assault has been a grievous part of human experience throughout history. For example, the Bible records a number of sexual assaults, both heterosexual and homosexual (Genesis 19; Genesis 34; Judges 19;

2 Samuel 13). Under Old Testament law, the penalty for sexual assault was death, "if out in the country a man happens to meet a girl pledged to be married and rapes her, only the man who has done this shall die. Do nothing to the girl; she has committed no sin deserving death. This case is like that of someone who attacks and murders his neighbor" (Deuteronomy 22:25–26). The victim was considered innocent.

Sexual assault statistics vary from country to country. In America,

- Every two minutes someone in the U.S. is sexually assaulted.
- 90% of victims are female, but males are attacked too.
- 73% of victims know their attackers, but strangers also attack.
- The incidence of sexual assault is highest for women under thirty, but people of all ages, from children to the elderly, may be attacked.[1]

Sexual assault can happen to anyone. But each person's case is unique. You are not a statistic. You are facing the aftermath of a grave evil. How does God meet you in the middle of this horrific experience? How do you recover? How do you rebuild?

Finding God in Your Struggle

Face what happened. This awful attack is now part of your life. You will be tempted to run from it, to deny it, to bury it, to keep yourself busy, to escape it, or to numb yourself. But it is crucial that you face what happened to you—your recovery depends on it. It's a part of your history and your life. Face what happened, but don't face it alone. God will take your hand. Other people can walk beside you. Your life is an unfolding story, and God doesn't erase or delete chapters. His redemption will be evident in this painful chapter also. Redemption begins with acknowledging what happened to you. God is "an ever-present help in trouble" (Psalm 46:1). Tell God all about this trouble. Say to him, "This is trouble. You are the Helper of the helpless. Help me!"

Face your reactions to what happened. You must be willing to enter your into your reactions. Something that is hurtful hurts. A violation makes you feel violated. Something that overpowers you makes you feel weak and overwhelmed. You need to be able to enter into your grief, hurt, confusion, fear, and anger. "My heart is in anguish within me" (Psalm 55:4). Tell God all about your anguish.

Face Jesus. Don't try to face what happened and your reactions to it by yourself. Invite Jesus into your struggle. Take hold of his promise of good: "When you pass through the waters, I will be with you; and when you pass through the rivers, they will not sweep over you. When you walk through the fire, you will not be burned; the flames will not set you ablaze" (Isaiah 43:2). You are walking in deep waters. God will walk with you. You are walking through fire. God will not let the flames consume you. Turn to him every day. Take God's promises to heart many times each day. Every time you remember, every time you struggle, every time you feel that your heart is breaking under the weight of what happened to you, ask him to help you.

Say his promises out loud, and then turn them into honest prayers. "You promise to be with me. I feel so alone. Please come to me. Please hold me up. Please help me." Speak them back to the One who is your hope. Having faith in Jesus is not something you do just once. He's the person toward whom you reach, to whom you cry, to whom you bring your pain, confusion, anger, fear, and need. He is the direction you face. He's the direction in which you live. He can bear the weight of your trouble and heartache. He also suffered at the hands of evil people. He knows how a broken body and a broken heart feel.

Pour out your heart to him. Say to him, "Help, Lord! Have mercy. I am in such need. You promise good to me. I feel such a weight of evil. Don't let me fear any evil. Make me know you are with me."

Learn to Trust God Again

Perhaps you always thought God would keep you safe. After your attack you feel like God didn't keep his promise to you. You may be wondering how you will ever learn to trust him again. Your questions run deep. If only knowing God made everything tidy and safe! But it is exactly in those places that are broken, dangerous, and hurtful that God meets his beloved children.

God calls Jesus, "My beloved Son." When Jesus was betrayed, tortured, and mocked he cried out,

> My God, my God, why have you forsaken me?
>> Why are you so far from saving me,
>> so far from the words of my groaning?
>
> (Psalm 22:1)

At the same time Jesus spoke these words on the cross, he knew that God does not treat our afflictions lightly and does not shrink back from our brokenness and need (Psalm 22:24). In his affliction Jesus trusts and cries out to God, "Into your hands I commit my spirit" (Luke 23:46). When you turn to God, he will give you the same spirit that Jesus had. He trusted God in the face of overwhelming tragedy, betrayal, and suffering. He did this for us. He entered into our sorrows to bear our sins. Trust that God can and will redeem even your most broken experiences. The questions you are facing now cannot be answered in a short paragraph. But they can be answered in a growing relationship of trust with the God who made you, who has loved you in the giving his own Son, and who has promised to be with you. Keep bringing your questions to him.

Ask others to pray with and for you as you struggle with these things. Make Romans 8:15-39 your own. A book I have found helpful in its discussion of suffering is *When God Weeps* by Joni Eareckson Tada and Steve Estes.[2]

Find Your Identity in Jesus

Often those who have been sexually assaulted feel a sense of shame. You may well feel unclean, as if you are now damaged goods. It's easy to let the ugly violation of your attack define you. But God makes beautiful what has been defaced. Because of Jesus you are cleansed and whole. Nothing that has happened or will happen can change that reality. This is how Isaiah expressed the joy of knowing his God-given identity:

> I will rejoice greatly in the LORD,
> My soul will exult in my God;
> For He has clothed me with garments of salvation,
> He has wrapped me with a robe of righteousness,
> As a bridegroom decks himself with a garland,
> And as a bride adorns herself with her jewels.
> (Isaiah 61:10 NASB)

Take hold of this picture. You were dirtied by another's violence. God clothes you with garments of light and beauty. You were polluted by another's garbage. God makes you clean in a robe of righteousness. You have been made beautiful, given pure white clothes, fragrant flowers, and fine gems. You don't necessarily feel like this. But God's reality runs deeper than the reality of evil.

Jesus made that picture a reality by giving himself for you on the cross. Seeking Jesus, trusting Jesus, he clothes you with himself—with his mercy, kindness, and goodness.

More Than a Survivor of Assault—Becoming a Servant of God

You might have heard that your identity should be that of a survivor instead of a victim. But "survivor" only means you've outlived something. If your ship goes down and you are rescued, then you survived the shipwreck. When your identity is that of survivor, you are still defined by what happened to you. What happened to you—the hateful person, the hateful thing that happened—still dominates your identity.

God's goal for you is bigger and better than mere survival. His goal for you is that you become his beloved servant. When you are God's servant, you are defined by his love for you, and that identity is profoundly liberating.

Your identity is not simply that you survived a dirty evil. You find yourself renewed in serving the beautiful One and being clothed with his beauty and goodness. Paul says that when we trust in God we are "clothed" with Christ (Romans 13:14; Galatians 3:27). You are defined by his love for you, not by the evil that someone else imposed on you.

Practical Strategies for Change

In the midst of extreme suffering, sometimes Jesus doesn't seem like "a present help." Instead, he seems distant and far away. If this is true for you, turn in his direction. Saying and singing God's truths out loud is one way for you to fill your mind and heart with comfort and hope.

For example, take the hymn "Jesus, What a Friend for Sinners." I've italicized all the parts of this hymn that speak of what happened to you.

> Jesus! What a Friend for sinners! Jesus! Lover of my soul;
>
> Friends may fail me, *foes assail me*, He, my Savior, makes me whole.
>
> Refrain: Hallelujah! What a Savior! Hallelujah! What a Friend!
>
> Saving, helping, keeping, loving, You are with me to the end.

Jesus! What a Strength *in weakness*! Let me hide myself in Him.

Tempted, tried, and sometimes failing, He, my Strength, my victory wins.

Jesus! What a Help *in sorrow! While the billows o'er me roll,*

Even when my heart is breaking, He, my Comfort, helps my soul.

Jesus! What a Guide and Keeper! *While the tempest still is high,*

Storms about me, night overtakes me, He, my Pilot, hears my cry.

Jesus! I do now receive You, More than all in You I find.

You have granted me forgiveness, I am yours, and you are mine.

Refrain: Hallelujah! What a Savior! Hallelujah! What a Friend!

>   Saving, helping, keeping, loving, You are with
> me to the end.

Use these words to express to Jesus what happened to you, how you felt, and how who Jesus is connects to you. This hymn expresses the experience of an intense, overwhelming attack: "foes assail me." It expresses feeling crushed and helpless: "while the billows o'er me roll." It expresses heartbreak: "even when my heart is breaking." It describes a pain that is too big to bear alone. Is this how you feel?

Jesus meets you right in the middle of this awful experience. You are "tempted, tried, and sometimes failing." But Jesus is your strength in weakness. He makes you whole. He helps you. He hears your cry. He is yours, and you are his. The assault has created great weakness and great trouble in your life. But as you turn to Jesus, you will find that he comes to you and strengthens you.

It's normal to struggle. It's okay to be weak. It's right to be troubled by trouble. Just make sure you are turning in Jesus' direction. What will you find as you turn to Jesus? You will find that he is your friend, the lover of your soul, your guide, your keeper. And what does he do? He saves, helps, keeps, and loves. He is with you to the end: "I am yours and you are mine." These are the truths about Jesus that invite a victim—that invite you—to come in his direction. When you feel crushed by your suffering, fill your mind and heart with this hymn. It is a hymn full of Jesus.

Bring Healing Love to Terrible Memories

Most likely you are struggling with vivid memories of the attack. Many people experience flashbacks of the attack. What happened to you is so dominating, so compelling, so traumatic, and so hurtful. It made a horrifying, deep impression. Ugly memories keep replaying over and over—like a video on an endless loop. How can your memories be transformed? The only way to deal with the video of your assault is to replace it with another video.

You might have been told to replace the video of your attack with mental relaxation techniques, perhaps imagining that you're on a sunny beach with gentle waves and safe people around you. But it is a losing battle to fight terrible realities with mere fantasies. Instead, God gives you a true video filled with his hope. He tells you of the invasion of earth by the Redeemer of the world. He will reckon justly with evil. He shows you how Jesus comes to you as a friend in the midst of your suffering.

Think of "Jesus, What a Friend for Sinners" as an alternative video. It's something you can think about, say out loud, and sing. When the video of foes assailing you starts playing, replace that with "Jesus, lover of my soul. Friends may fail me, foes assail me. He, my Savior, makes me whole. Hallelujah! What a Savior! Saving, helping, keeping, loving, you are with me to the end."

This isn't magic. It's a conversation with the one person who can help. There's no guarantee that you can easily erase the old tape of your attack and replace it with the friendship of Jesus. Building a friendship is a process that takes time. But you can learn to answer back to the traumatic video of your attack and call out to the God of goodness and grace. As you do this, memories of the terrible thing that happened to you will actually lead you to take hold of Jesus. He befriends you in the midst of the worst experience of your life.

Replace Bitterness with Forgiveness

Forgiveness is another crucial step. Going in Jesus' direction means taking seriously his call to do two things that seem contradictory: hate what is evil; forgive from your heart.

- "Hate what is evil; cling to what is good." (Romans 12:9)
- "If you hold anything against anyone, forgive him." (Mark 11:25)

How do you do both? It's likely that the attacker will never ask you for forgiveness. You aren't forgiving him human to human. But how can you be delivered from the poisons of bitterness, hatred, and fear? You are forgiving him before God, so that you will not return evil for evil (Romans 12:17).

Jesus says you should forgive "when you stand praying" (Mark 11:25). You are forgiving in God's presence, not face-to-face with the person who betrayed you. Your goal is to pursue an attitude of forgiveness in your heart before God toward the attacker.

What happened to you was a great evil. Forgiveness won't come easily or in a moment. It will be a journey of many small steps. The alternatives to forgiveness are fear, escapism, bitterness, numbness, and depression. When you live like this, evil still controls you. Forgiveness frees you to live a life of love towards God and others. Forgiveness frees you to be a servant.

Often those who have suffered a great evil think that forgiveness means excusing the evil. So before we talk about forgiving your attacker, let's talk about what forgiveness does *not* mean:

- Forgiveness *does not mean* that what happened to you was "okay" or can be excused.
- Forgiveness *does not mean* that what happened to you was a small, unimportant thing.
- Forgiveness *does not mean* you will forget what happened to you.
- Forgiveness *does not mean* you shouldn't seek to have the perpetrator justly punished by the law and put where he cannot harm others.

What Forgiveness Does Mean

Forgiveness says what happened was wrong, destructive, cruel, and inexcusable, but you are choosing to not take personal vengeance. Why not? Because God says, "Never take your own revenge, beloved, but leave room for the wrath of God, for it is written, 'Vengeance is mine, I will repay,' says the Lord" (Romans 12:19 NASB). And God has shown mercy to you (Romans 12:1).

What happened to you was worthy of hate. Yet if you become consumed with hatred and vengeful fantasies, then you are acting in your heart like a killer. When you repay evil for evil, you are stealing God's role in the universe and becoming a vengeance-taker. Forgiveness leaves your attacker in God's hands. It trusts him to make every wrong right. It is grateful for his mercies toward you.

Remember God's Mercy to You

Perhaps you know you should forgive, but you are stuck in bitterness and rage. What can you do? Start by remembering God's mercy to you: "Jesus! What a friend for sinners! Jesus! Lover of my soul!" Jesus chose to enter a world of violence, and chose to die for your sins. Part of your liberation from the devastating effects of sexual assault comes as you see your own need for mercy. God's love and forgiveness for you, in Christ, is deeper, bigger, and longer lasting than what you have suffered.

True forgiveness for a true evil is only possible because of God's forgiveness of you. Paul explains it like this: "Be kind and compassionate to one another, forgiving each other, just as in Christ God forgave you" (Ephesians 4:32).

Here are some truths that will help you remember God's mercies to you:

1. *Think vertically, not horizontally.* Don't line up your sins next to how you were sinned against. Don't compare them trying to see if they are equal. That's not the scale God uses. No one would ever be able to forgive an atrocity, unless they had done something equally terrible! With rare exceptions, the victims of sexual assault are far "more sinned against than sinning."[3] The victims of heinous crimes would be forever stuck in bitterness and hatred if the only way they could forgive would be if they'd been forgiven for equally detestable crimes. So *how* can you ever

forgive a grave evil? Think vertically. "But God, being rich in mercy, because of His great love with which He loved us, even when we were dead in our transgressions, made us alive together with Christ (by grace you have been saved)" (Ephesians 2:4–5 NASB). While we were still weak, while we were ungodly, while we were still sinners, while we were enemies, Christ died for us to reconcile us to God (Romans 5:6–10). Your need for mercy from God operates on a whole different scale from the wrongs that one human being does to another. This does not trivialize the evils you experience. God never says, "Oh, that's nothing." The experience of betrayal and violence is so terrible that it was in Jesus' own heart to say, "My heart is in anguish within me, and the terrors of death have fallen upon me. Fear and trembling come upon me, and horror has overwhelmed me" (Psalm 55:4–5 NASB). But Jesus came on a mission to forgive people whose need for forgiveness runs deep—and you're included among the needy. He brought mercy rather than just vengeance: "Father, forgive them." Jesus is still on that mission.

He forgives you in order to remake you like himself, a woman or man able to forgive great wrongs.

2. *Identify the destructive ways you are responding to the attack.* Are you responding with escapist behavior—using alcohol, drugs, food, sleep, shopping, or something else? With denial and numbness? Your reactions come from inside of you, and they reveal what masters you. What do your reactions reveal? Are you being ruled by fear? Seething hatred and bitterness? Unbelief that tries to erase God and run from him? These reactions to what you have suffered are common. Of course there is a just sense of shock and fear and anger, a just desire that pain would go away. We are human beings, not stones. But destructive and self-destructive reactions are exaggerations and distortions. They are not meant to rule your life. You are living in God's world. He is meant to be the ruler of your heart, even when (especially when) the world seems to be collapsing around you. So when you recognize that you are struggling with destructive reactions to your attack,

it's your opportunity to remember how much you need mercy and how much you need to ask God for forgiveness. He is merciful. He truly is.

3. *Identify false guilt.* Your mind may be filled with an avalanche of "if only," "it's all my fault," and "why did I do this?" Probably 95 percent of these feelings will be false or distorted. You do not need forgiveness for these. The attacker's actions were not your fault. They were his fault. Bring all of your confusion and hurt to God and cast it all on him. "Cast all your anxiety on him because he cares for you" (1 Peter 5:7). Often it's helpful to talk with someone who will reassure you that guilty feelings are not always true.

4. *Ask God to forgive you for any wrong choices.* If you sinned in the process leading up to the assault, it is freeing to name what happened and ask God for forgiveness. Hear me rightly on this point. What happened to you was criminal. Remember that no matter what you did, you are not responsible for someone else's sin against you. You are only responsible for what you did. God makes it very clear in

the Bible that each person is responsible for his or her own actions (James 1:14–15). If there are things troubling your conscience, bring these to God. Perhaps a previous relationship with your attacker crossed sexual lines. Perhaps you placed yourself in a compromising position, acted in a sexually provocative manner, or got drunk. God promises forgiveness to everyone who asks (1 John 1:7–9). If you are having trouble sorting out true guilt from false, ask a wise friend or pastor for help.

Talk with People You Trust

God does not intend for you to face your heartbreak alone. One of the ways he helps you is through other people. You cannot solve this deep problem privately and alone. Find someone (or a group of people) you trust. Talk and pray with them.

This might not be easy. Some of your friends won't know how to handle the aftermath of your attack. They might avoid you. Or they might say things that make you feel even worse. Ask God to help you forgive your friends if they say foolish things or act in ways that are uncaring or hurtful. Offer them the same forgiveness and mercy you have received from God.

Wise friends will love you well, hang in there with you, point you to Jesus, and talk to you candidly and tenderly. If you don't have friends like this, ask God to provide them for you. And then look for a church community where you can get connected.

Give Your Renewal Time

Sometimes people talk about "recovery" from a terrible experience. But "recovery" means getting back to what was. It's better to think about the process you are in as "renewal." Having faced terrible evil, you grow through it into a person with deeper, wiser faith. You grow through it into a person with a deeper love and a greater ability to enter into the troubles and struggles of others. There is no timetable. Take the time you need.

This terrible, traumatic evil happened in a moment (or repeated incidents), but dealing with the consequences and finding the ways that God will meet you and grow you will take time. And there are tears that will not be wiped away until the last day (Revelation 21:1–5). Some aspects of your pain may not be fully removed until Jesus comes again and heals all things. But there is also a genuine healing process, a genuine growing process, a genuine transforming process. Something that is a terrible evil can be changed into something that brings about good in your life and in the lives of others. That process takes time.

Be a Servant to Others

When your identity is that of a servant of Jesus Christ (the "Servant of servants"), you are able to move toward others with love, even in the midst of your suffering. As you live out your identity as God's servant, you will find that there are people who will need your help. This is one of the ways God works long-term good out of moments of extreme evil (Genesis 50:20). There are other men, women, and children who have gone through similar experiences or other sorts of painful trouble. It's no accident that people who come to terms with an evil like this often become useful in the lives of others. You are able to combine compassion for the terrible trouble they're going through with a clear-mindedness about the way forward. Just living your life well will bring hope to others who are suffering that there's a way forward. You can share how this process can come out good, even though it's dark and overwhelming right at the moment.

As you do this, you are passing on the comfort you received from God to others. As Paul put it, "Praise be to the God and Father of our Lord Jesus Christ, the Father of compassion and the God of all comfort, who comforts us in all our troubles, so that we can comfort those in any trouble with the comfort we ourselves have received from God" (2 Corinthians 1:3–4).

I have counseled many people who have suffered through extreme hardship. After going through the process of facing their hardship and facing Jesus, they invariably say something like this, "I would never want to go through that again; it was evil and dark. But I would never trade what I've learned about the love of Jesus and his grace in the midst of my suffering." As you walk through this hard time—struggling in Jesus' direction—God will give you that same perspective.

Endnotes

1 Statistics quoted by RAINN (Rape, Abuse and Incest National Network), http://www.rainn.org/statistics.
2 Joni Eareckson Tada and Steve Estes, *When God Weeps* (Grand Rapids: Zondervan, 1997).
3 Shakespeare, *King Lear*, 3:2. References are to act and scene.